HAPPY CHRISTMAS

GEORGE

LOVE DAD xxx

Published by Century in 2005

1 3 5 7 9 10 8 6 4 2

Copyright is for losers©™

Previously published in part as three small little books.

First published in the United Kingdom in 2005 by Century, The Random House Group Limited , 20 Vauxhall Bridge Road, London SW1V 2SA. Random House Australia (Pty) Limited, 20 Alfred Street, Milsons Point, Sydney, New South Wales 2061, Australia. Random House, New Zealand Limited, 18 Poland Road, Glenfield, Auckland 10, New Zealand. Random House South Africa (Pty) Limited, Endulini, 5a Jubilee Road, Parktown 2193, South Africa.

The Random House Group Limited Reg. No. 954009. www.randomhouse.co.uk. A CIP catalogue record for this book is available from the British Library. Papers used by Random House are natural, recyclable products made from wood grown insustainable forests. The manufacturing processes conform to the environmental regulations of the country of origin

ISBN 1844137864

Printed and bound in Germany by Appl Druck, Wemding

Note from the publisher: This book shows the creative/artistic element of graffiti art and is not meant to encourage or induce graffiti where it is illegal or inappropriate.

Wall and Piece

12 minutes, Bankside, London 2001

I'm going to speak my mind, so this won't take very long.

Graffiti is not the lowest form of art. Despite having to creep about at night and lie to your mum it's actually the most honest artform available. There is no elitism or hype, it exhibits on some of the best walls a town has to offer, and nobody is put off by the price of admission.

A wall has always been the best place to publish your work.

The people who run our cities don't understand graffiti because they think nothing has the right to exist unless it makes a profit. But if you just value money then your opinion is worthless.

They say graffiti frightens people and is symbolic of the decline in society, but graffiti is only dangerous in the mind of three types of people; politicians, advertising executives and graffiti writers.

The people who truly deface our neighbourhoods are the companies that scrawl their giant slogans across buildings and buses trying to make us feel inadequate unless we buy their stuff. They expect to be able to shout their message in your face from every available surface but you're never allowed to answer back. Well, they started this fight and the wall is the weapon of choice to hit them back.

Some people become cops because they want to make the world a better place. Some people become vandals because they want to make the world a better *looking* place.

All artists are prepared to suffer for their work

When I was eighteen I spent one night trying to paint 'LATE AGAIN' in big silver bubble letters on the side of a passenger train. British transport police showed up and I got ripped to shreds running away through a thorny bush. The rest of my mates made it to the car and disappeared so I spent over an hour hidden under a dumper truck with engine oil leaking all over me. As I lay there listening to the cops on the tracks I realised I had to cut my painting time in half or give up altogether. I was staring straight up at the stencilled plate on the bottom of a fuel tank when I realised I could just copy that style and make each letter three feet high.

I got home at last and crawled into bed next to my girlfriend. I told her I'd had an epiphany that night and she told me to stop taking that drug cos it's bad for your heart.

Nobody ever listened to me until they didn't know who I was.

You're no safer in first class. 20 minutes, District Line, London 2002

Simple intelligence testing

A lot of people never use their initiative because no-one told them to

Broken Window Theory

Criminologists James Q Wilson and George Kelling developed a theory of criminal behaviour in the 1980's that became known as the 'Broken Window Theory'. They argued crime was the inevitable result of disorder and that if a window in a building is smashed but not repaired people walking by will think no-one cares. Then more windows will be broken, graffiti will appear and rubbish get dumped. The likelihood of serious crime being committed then increases dramatically as neglect becomes visible. The researchers believed there was a direct link between vandalism, street violence and the general decline of society. This theory was the basis of the infamous New York City crime purge of the early nineties and the zero-tolerance attitude to graffiti.

Letter received to Banksy website

I dont know who you are or how many of you there are but i am writing to ask you to stop painting your things where we live. In particular xxxxxx road in Hackney. My brother and me were born here and have lived here all our lives but these days so many yuppies and students are moving here neither of us can afford to buy a house where we grew up anymore. Your graffities are undoubtably part of what makes these wankers think our area is cool. You're obviously not from round here and after youve driven up the house prices youll probably just move on. Do us all a favour and go do your stuff somewhere else like Brixton.

daniel (name and address not witheld)

Angel, London 2004

Naples, Brick Lane, Bristol,
Paris, Berlin, Brighton, Mexico

Speak softly, but carry a big can of paint. Mona Lisa with rocket launcher. 15 minutes, Soho 2001. Later converted to Osama Bin Laden by an unknown artist. Then removed after two days.

Brighton 2003

I like to think I have the guts to stand up anonymously in a western democracy and call for things no-one else believes in – like peace and justice and freedom.

Vienna 2003

Some people represent authority
without ever possessing any of their own

There are no exceptions to the rule that
everyone thinks they're an exception to the rules

Shoreditch, London 2003. Modified face by unknown artist

Shoreditch, London 2004

Portobello Road, London 2002

Shoreditch, London 2002

Clerkenwell, London 2003

HAVE A NICE DAY

FRANCO'S FISH & CHIPS
G
Tel 0171· 253 7764
TAKEAWAY

CHIPS
AY

Happy Chopper, Shoreditch 2003. Special effects supplied by deep fat fryer

Ring road (W)
(A1, A400, A41)

The City
West End
Holborn

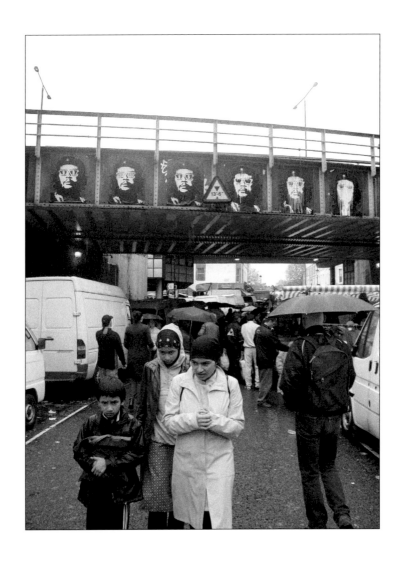

This revolution is for display purposes only

On a Tuesday night in the summer I tried to paint a train bridge that spans Portobello Road in West London with posters showing the revolutionary leader Che Guevara gradually dribbling off the page. Every Saturday the market underneath the bridge sells Che Guevara t-shirts, handbags, baby bibs and button badges. I think I was trying to make a statement about the endless recycling of an icon by endlessly recycling an icon.

People seem to think if they dress like a revolutionary they don't actually have to behave like one.

I got up on the bridge about 4am. It was quiet and peaceful until two cars approached very slowly and parked on the street. I stopped pasting and watched from the side of the bridge through the bushes. After a few minutes there was no movement and I figured it was cool to carry on.

I reached the fifth poster when there was a huge bang and the sound of splitting wood. One of the cars had reversed back up the street and was on the pavement, wedged in the doorway of the mobile phone shop. Six small figures in hoods with scarves over their faces ran into the store throwing everything they could into black plastic bags. In less than a minute they were all back in their cars which screamed down Portobello Road beneath me. I stood there with my mouth hanging open, a bucket in one hand and a sawn-off sweeping brush in the other. Being the only young male in sportswear within a mile I got the feeling things would look bad for me if I hung around so I dropped the bucket, climbed the fence and jumped to the street.

The area was full of cameras so I lowered my head, pulled my hood up and ran all the way to the canal. I imagined the kids were probably in Kilburn by then, lighting up a spliff and saying to each other 'Why would someone just paint pictures of a revolutionary when you can actually behave like one instead?'

The corrupt and brutal regime of President Ceausescu of Romania was infamous across the world. His ferocious government had run the country emphatically for many years, crushing any signs of dissent ruthlessly. In November 1989 he was re-elected President for another five years as his supporters at Party Conference gave him forty standing ovations.

On December 21st the President, disturbed by a small uprising in the western city of Timisoara in support of a Protestant Clergyman, was persuaded to address a public rally in Bucharest.

One solitary man in the crowd, Nica Leon, sick to death with Ceausescu and the dreadful circumstances he created for everyone started shouting in favour of the revolutionaries in Timasoara. The crowd around him, obedient to the last, thought that when he shouted out 'long live Timisoara!' it was some new political slogan.

They started chanting it too. It was only when he called, 'Down with Ceausescu!' that they realised something wasn't quite right. Terrified, they tried to force themselves away from him, dropping the banners they had been carrying. In the crush the wooden batons on which the banners were held began to snap underfoot and women started screaming. The ensuing panic sounded like booing.

The unthinkable was happening. Ceausescu stood there on his balcony, ludicrously frozen in uncertainty, his mouth opening and shutting. Even the official camera shook with fright. Then the head of security walked swiftly acrosss the balcony towards him and whispered, 'They're getting in'. It was clearly audible on the open microphone and was broadcast over the whole country on live national radio.

This was the start of the revolution. Within a week Ceausescu was dead.

Source: John Simpson BBC News

Bristol Fashion

Wearing your jeans two sizes too big
so they hang low off your ass in a
gangsta fashion was invented in Los
Angeles. The kids wear clothes
handed down by their brothers so
the bigger the trousers, the bigger
your brothers.

This makes sense until you wear
your slacks this way to go fountain
painting. If they get damp they tend
to fall down halfway through the
piece. Then you have to wait for a
night bus looking like you've just
pissed all over yourself. It doesn't
matter how big your brothers are
when drunk geezers walk past and
see that.

Council House, Bristol 2001

One night I painted the side of a
floating night club in Bristol.
Apparently the owner quite liked it so
when the harbour manager ordered it
to be painted over the club
threatened legal action. They never
pursued it any further so I went out
and hit it again in the hope I could
lure the harbour manager out for a full
custodial sentence this time.

Once upon a time, there was a king who ruled a great and glorious nation. Favourite amongst his subjects was the court painter of whom he was very proud. Everybody agreed this wizzened old man painted the greatest pictures in the whole kingdom and the king would spend hours each day gazing at them in wonder.

However, one day a dirty and dishevelled stranger presented himself at the court claiming that in fact *he* was the greatest painter in the land. The indignant king decreed a competition would be held between the two artists, confident it would teach the vagabond an embarrassing lesson. Within a month they were both to produce a masterpiece that would out do the other.

After thirty days of working feverishly day and night, both artists were ready. They placed their paintings, each hidden by a cloth, on easels in the great hall of the castle. As a large crowd gathered, the king ordered the cloth to be pulled first from the court artist's easel. Everyone gasped as before them was revealed a wonderful oil painting of a table set with a feast. At its centre was an ornate silver bowl full of exotic fruits glistening moistly in the dawn light. As the crowd gazed admiringly, a sparrow perched high up on the rafters of the hall swooped down and hungrily tried to snatch one of the grapes from the painted bowl only to hit the canvas and fall down dead with shock at the feet of the king.

'Aha!' exclaimed the king. 'My artist has produced a painting so

wonderful it has fooled Nature herself, surely you must agree that he is the greatest painter who ever lived!' But the vagabond said nothing and stared solemnly at his feet. 'Now, pull the blanket from your painting and let us see what you have for us,' cried the king. But the tramp remained motionless and said nothing. Growing impatient, the king stepped forward and reached out to grab the blanket only to freeze in horror at the last moment.

'You see,' said the tramp quietly, 'there is no blanket covering the painting. This is actually just a painting of a cloth covering a painting. And whereas your famous artist is content to fool Nature, I've made the king of the whole country look like a clueless little twat'.

Source: man in a pub

BY ORDER
NATIONAL HIGHWAYS AGENCY

THIS WALL IS A DESIGNATED
GRAFFITI AREA

PLEASE TAKE YOUR LITTER HOME
EC REF. URBA 23/366

The greatest crimes in the world are not committed by people breaking the rules but by people who follow orders that drop bombs and massacre villages.

As a precaution to ever committing major acts of evil it is our solemn duty never to do what we're told, this is the only way we can be sure.

Day 1

Day 9

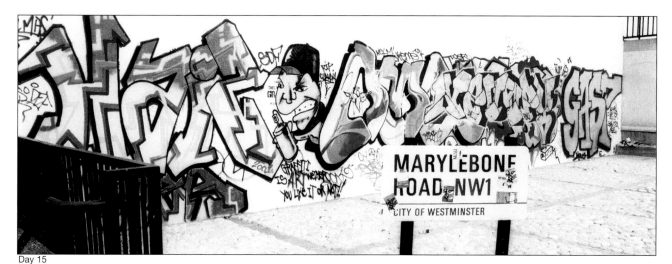

Day 15

email received to banksy website

I was one of the writers that fell for your 'legal' graffiti site thingy-ma-bob on marylebone street next to edgeware rd. i write AMBS SDF. i was there with gasp zeal and haze when we pieced it. you know we got nicked for it at the end of the day when we had finished by an undercover fed, but he let us go because before we had started we asked at the fed station across the road if it realy was legal and they said it was cool. anyway it was all good at the end and we got some nice pieces in a fuckin bait plot. mail me back if you want, anyway....... peace!

Day 1

Day 18

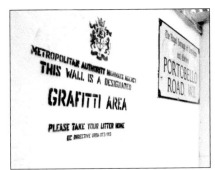

Day 1

First attempt (complete with incorrect spelling of graffiti and a crest taken off a fag packet).

Day 25

Day 34

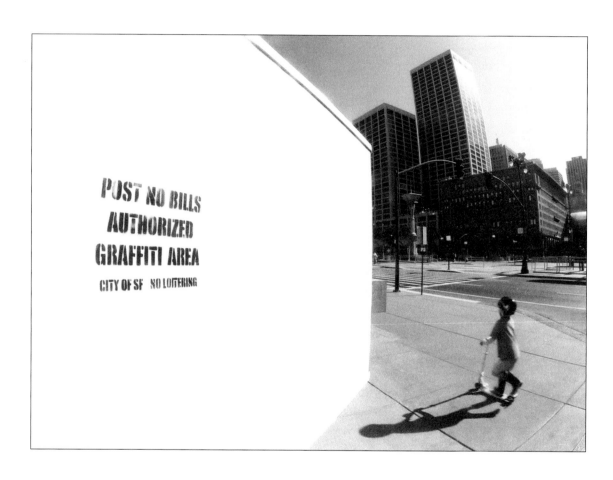

POST NO BILLS
AUTHORIZED
GRAFFITI AREA
CITY OF SF   NO LOITERING

On Tuesday I went round San Francisco in the middle of the day dressed in overalls designating parts of it as legal graffiti areas.

By Friday a lot had been modified by city workers who simply removed the offending part with a lick of paint.

POST NO BILLS

CITY OF SF   NO LOITERING

DESIGNATED
PICNIC AREA
⬇

Hackney, London 2004

Four minutes, Trafalgar Square, London 2003

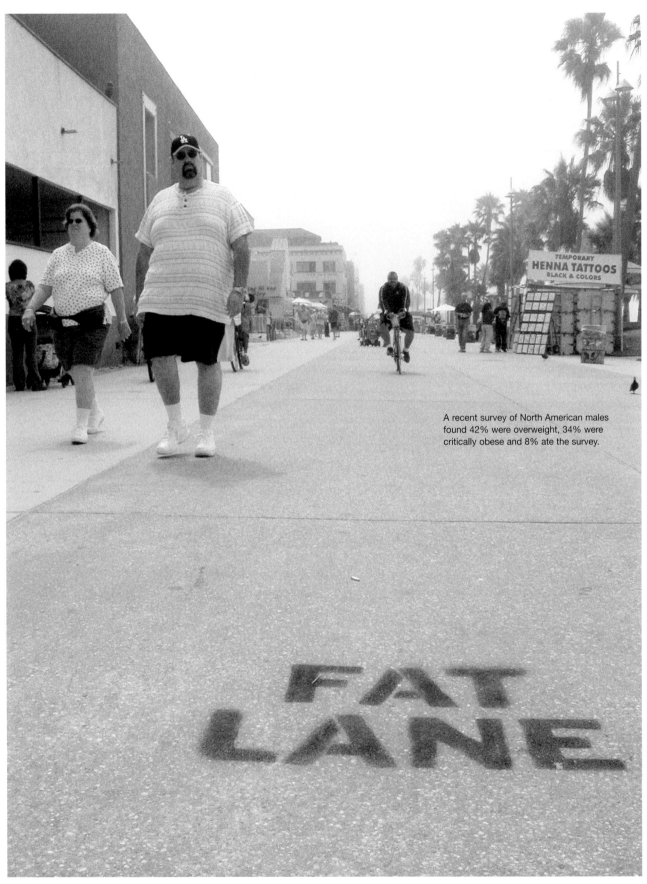

A recent survey of North American males found 42% were overweight, 34% were critically obese and 8% ate the survey.

Venice Beach, California 2003

Millenium Bridge, London 2002

Bethnal Green, London 2002

Brighton Beach 2004

Weston Super Mare 2003

Barcelona 2003

Soho, London 2004

Southbank, London 2004

When the time comes to leave, just walk away quietly and don't make any fuss

Notting Hill, London 2005

Once upon a time there was a Bear and a Bee who lived in a wood and were the best of friends. All summer long the Bee collected nectar from morning to night while the Bear lay on his back basking in the long grass.

When Winter came the Bear realised he had nothing to eat and thought to himself 'I hope that busy little Bee will share some of his honey with me'. But the Bee was nowhere to be found – he had died of a stress induced coronary disease

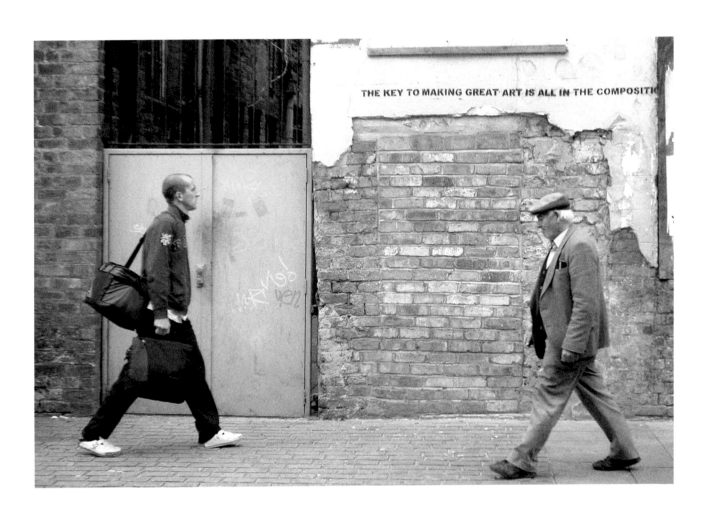

THE KEY TO MAKING GREAT ART IS ALL IN THE COMPOSITIO

Liverpool 2004

Brick Lane, London 2005

Nothing dispels enthusiasm like a small admission fee. Garage wall in Highbury 2004

Tate Gallery, London 2002

WHAT ARE
YOU
LOOKING AT?

Marble Arch, London 2004

Manchester 2002

'Art is all about finding the paint-job that turned the donkey into the zebra' an old man on a cider farm told me.

Quarry at Dead Woman's Bottom, Somerset 2004

Painting something that defies the law of the
land is good. Painting something that defies the
law of the land and the law of gravity at the
same time is ideal.

Hackney, London 2003

They exist without permission. They are hated, hunted and persecuted. They live in quiet desperation amongst the filth. And yet they are capable of bringing entire civilsations to their knees.

If you are dirty, insignificant and unloved then rats are the ultimate role model.

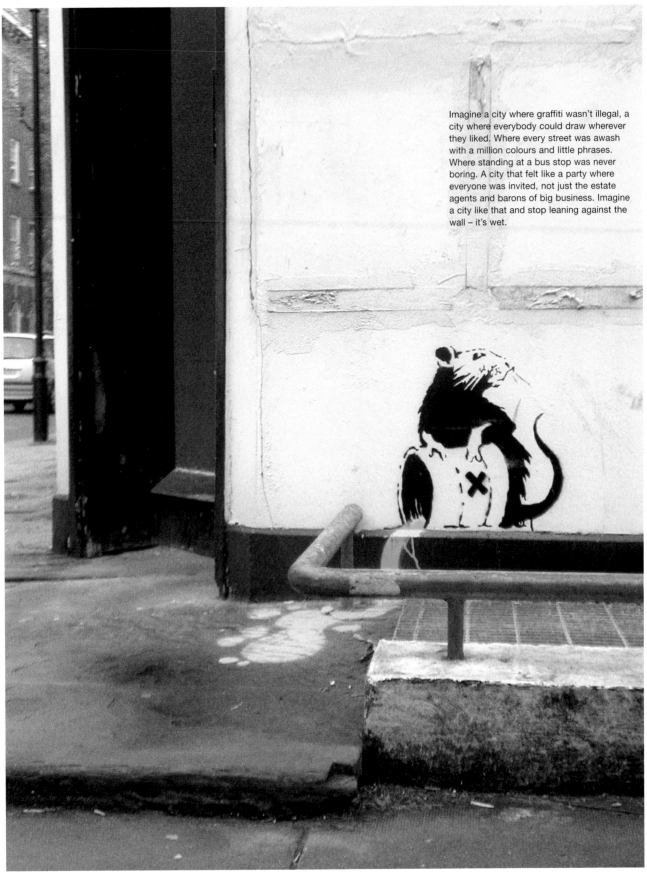

Imagine a city where graffiti wasn't illegal, a city where everybody could draw wherever they liked. Where every street was awash with a million colours and little phrases. Where standing at a bus stop was never boring. A city that felt like a party where everyone was invited, not just the estate agents and barons of big business. Imagine a city like that and stop leaning against the wall – it's wet.

I'd been painting rats for three years before someone said 'that's clever it's an anagram of art' and I had to pretend I'd known that all along.

You can win the rat race but you're still a rat.

The human race is an unfair and stupid competition. A lot of the runners don't even get decent sneakers or clean drinking water.

Some runners are born with a massive head start, every possible help along the way and still the referees seem to be on their side.

It's not surprising a lot of people have given up competing altogether and gone to sit in the grandstand, eat junk food and shout abuse.

What we need in this race is a lot more streakers.

The Ritz, Picadilly 2005

Angel, London 2005

When I was nine years old I was expelled from school. It was punishment for swinging one of my classmates round and round before dropping him onto a concrete floor. He was taken away from school by an ambulance that had to pull right into the playground and pick him up on a stretcher.

The next day I was made to stand in front of the whole school at assembly while the headmaster gave a speech about good and evil before I was sent home in disgrace.

The unfortunate part is that I never actually touched the kid. It was my best friend Jimmy who had put him into casualty. Me and a boy called Martin watched Jimmy grab the kid's hand and swing him until he was too dizzy to stand up and when he let go the kid just seemed to fly off and land on his head. It wasn't even malicious, just stupid. However, Jim was a big chap for his age and could be very persuasive. So when we noticed the kid wasn't getting up Jim convinced Martin to say that it

was me who had done it. The only other witness was the kid himself who didn't regain conciousness for a week.

I tried many times to explain that I hadn't done it, but the boys stuck to their story. Eventually my mum turned to me and said bitterly that I should have the guts to admit when I was wrong and that it was even more disgusting when I refused to accept what I'd done.

So I shut up after that.

The kid sustained a fractured skull and some mental problems. He couldn't remember how it had happened and he didn't return to school for a long time.

I think I was lucky to learn so young that there's no point in behaving yourself. You'll be punished for something you never did anyway. People get it wrong all the time.

Anyone who believes in capital punishment should be shot.

West London 2002

Cashpoint with Di-Faced Tenners, Farringdon, London 2005

Conversations don't get any better as you get older

Deptford, London 2004

Columbia Road, London 2004

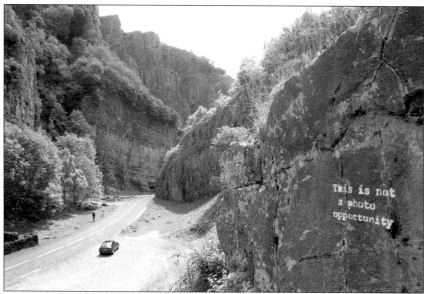

Tourism is not a spectator sport. Sydney, Paris, Cheddar

It's the middle of the night and we're on the bridge facing Shoreditch police station, home to the SO19 firearms unit, painting a seventy foot wide bank of riot cops brandishing shooters with smiley faces. In a window of an office overlooking the bridge is a bloke working at a computer so we have to work quietly.

After twenty minutes we've reached the part of the bridge very near the offices and I realise the bloke is at the window, cupping his hands to his eyes and squinting out. He's clocked what's going and opens the window shouting 'Hey, Hey!' I wonder if he works for the magistrates court attached to the police station and start to pack up the kit.

'I want a word with you' he shouts through the gap in the window 'About what?' I say, collapsing the brush and stepping back, we're nearly ready to roll.

There's a pause. 'Well, you see, I'm making a documentary about street culture and I'd like you to be in it…' We burst out laughing and shout in unison 'Fucking Shoreditch,' finish the piece and leave before he has a chance to get his camera out.

Policemen and security guards wear hats with a peak that comes down low over their eyes. Apparently this is for psychological reasons. Eyebrows are very expressive and you appear a lot more authoritative if you keep them covered up.

The advantage of this is that it makes it a lot harder for cops to see anything more than six foot off the ground. Which is why painting rooftops and bridges is so easy.

Murder Mile, Hackney, London 2003

Hackney, London 2004

Archway, London 2004

Holborn, London 2004

Segregation Wall, Palestine

Palestine has been occupied by the Israeli army since 1967. In 2002 the Israeli government began building a wall separating the occupied territories from Israel, much of it illegal under international law. It is controlled by a series of checkpoints and observation towers, stands three times the height of the Berlin wall and will eventually run for over 700km – the distance from London to Zurich. Palestine is now the world's largest open-air prison and the ultimate activity holiday destination for graffiti artists.

Bethlehem 2005

My guide   *You could paint here – there are no guards in the watch towers, they do not come until the winter.*

Me   *(Returning to the car after painting for 25 minutes) What's so funny?*

Guide   *(Lauging hysterically) Of course the guards are in the towers, they have the snipers with the walkie-talkies.*

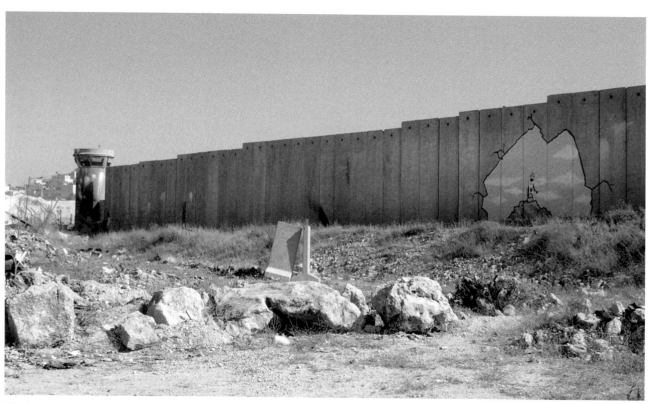

35 minutes in two visits. Ramallah checkpoint.

Old man	*You paint the wall, you make it look beautiful*
Me	*Thanks*
Old man	*We don't want it to be beautiful, we hate this wall, go home*

Bethlehem checkpoint

Abu Dis

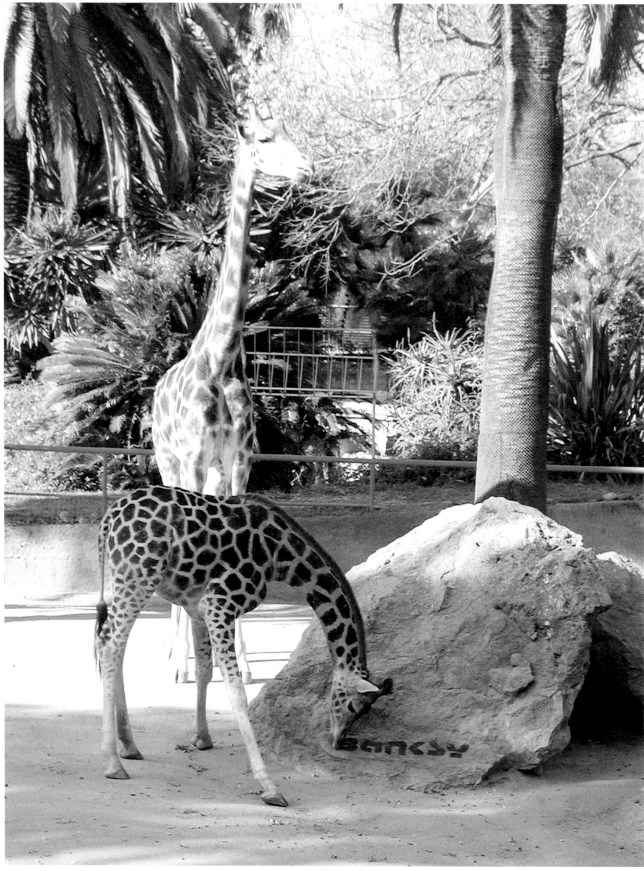

Zoo painting

I jumped the fence into central park, Barcelona, at three o'clock in the morning but didn't realise the park which houses the zoo is also home to the Catalan parliament. Its exceptionally well lit and patrolled by Guardia Civil in high-powered jeeps.

I was creeping across the edge of the park when a patrol took me by surprise and I dived into the shrubbery a bit too late.

The jeep pulled to a stop and didn't move for a long time. In my mind I was forming a story about how I was a penniless traveller with no hotel room sleeping rough in the park, and that I always carried 12 cans of spraypaint, a climbing rope and stencils with me. Then I heard footsteps approaching from the fence directly behind me

The fear was properly on me as I held my breath, parted the ivy leaves, and came eyeball to eyeball with an enormous fucking kangaroo.

I tried to relax by staring out the marsupial and after a few minutes the Guardia jeep started up and drove away across the park. Within five minutes I had climbed both fences and was inside the zoo.

British zoos have pictures of the animals on a board at the front of each enclosure. Barcelona Zoo doesn't do this so I was taking extra care before entering each pen. I was moving at speed putting up tags on the penguin, giraffe, bison and gazelle enclosures before reaching my ultimate destination – the elephant house.

A Spanish kid had translated 'Laugh now but one day we'll be in charge' for me on a small piece of paper. I got the paint out ready to write this in three foot high animal-like handwriting across the back wall, only to find I no longer had the piece of paper. Crouching next to a huge pile of dung my mind froze up. I can order lager in Spanish but not much else. I couldn't even think of how you would write 'Help us' in any language other than English but that seemed a bit rude. I checked my watch for the fifteenth time and then figured this was my best option – ticking off the time in classic jailhouse style |||| |||| |||| ||||.

I weighed in five cans of fat black, scrawling this over every available surface of the entire enclosure. Then crept away quietly.

By the time I got up the following afternoon I didn't get any photos of the elephant enclosure. Emergency cleaners had been working hard on it and covered up the rest with plastic sheeting. It's frustrating when the only people with good photos of your work are the police department.

Longleat Safari Park 2003

Melbourne Zoo 2003

GIVE WAY
150 yds

Hick Hop

If you grow up in a town where they don't have subway trains you have to find something else to graffiti.

It's not as easy as it sounds because most subway train drivers don't wander around with shotguns.

Vandalised oil paintings

If you want to survive as a graffiti writer when you go indoors your only option is to carry on painting over things that don't belong to you there either.

'Crimewatch UK has ruined the countryside for all of us'
2003 Oil on canvas

This new acquisition is a beautiful example of the neo post-idiotic style. The Artist has found an unsigned oil painting in a London street market and then stenciled Police incident tape over the top. It can be argued that defacing such an idyllic scene reflects the way our nation has been vandalised by its obsession with crime and paedophilia, where any visit to a secluded beauty spot now feels like it may result in being molested or finding discarded body parts.

Presented by the artist personally 2003

Making an exhibition of yourself

My sister threw away loads of my drawings when I was a kid and when I asked her where they were she shrugged and said 'Well it's not like they're ever gonna be hanging in the Louvre is it?'

Installation in the Louvre, Paris 2004
Duration unknown

Become good at cheating and you never need
to become good at anything else

Art is not like other culture because its success is not made by its audience. The public fill concert halls and cinemas every day, we read novels by the millions and buy records by the billions. We the people, affect the making and the quality of most of our culture, but not our art.

The Art we look at is made by only a select few. A small group create, promote, purchase, exhibit and decide the success of Art. Only a few hundred people in the world have any real say. When you go to an Art gallery you are simply a tourist looking at the trophy cabinet of a few millionaires.

Original artist unknown. Modified oil painitng installed Brooklyn Museum 2005. Lasted 8 days

After sticking up the picture I took five minutes
to watch what happened next. A sea of people
walked up, stared and left looking confused and
slightly cheated. I felt like a true modern artist.

Withus Oragainstus

United States

Pest Control

Recently discovered specimens of the
common sewer rat have shown some
remarkable new characteristics.

Attributed to an increase in junk food waste,
ambient radiation and hardcore urban rap
music these creatures have evolved at an
unprecedented rate. Termed the Banksus
Militus Vandalus they are impervious to all
modern methods of pest control and mark
their territory with a series of elaborate signs.

Professor B. Langford of University College
London states "You can laugh now... but one
day they may be in charge."

TV has made going to the theatre seem pointless, photography has pretty much killed painting, but graffiti remains gloriously unspoilt by progress.

Wall art
East London

This finely preserved example of primitive art dates from the Post-Catatonic era and is thought to depict early man venturing towards the out-of-town hunting grounds. The artist responsible is known to have created a substantial body of work across the South East of England under the moniker Banksymus Maximus but little else is known about him. Most art of this type has unfortunately not survived. The majority is destroyed by zealous municipal officials who fail to recognise the artistic merit and historical value of daubing on walls.

PRB 17752,2-2,1

Sometimes I feel so sick at the state of the world I can't even finish my second apple pie

Brandalism

People abuse you everyday. They butt into your life, take a cheap shot at you and then disappear. They leer at you from tall buildings and make you feel small. They make flippant comments from buses that imply you're not sexy enough and that all the fun is happening somewhere else. They're on TV making your girlfriend feel inadequate. They have access to the most sophisticated technology the world has ever seen and they bully you with it. They are The Advertisers and they are laughing at you.

However, you are forbidden to touch them. Trademarks, intellectual property rights and copyright law mean advertisers can say what they like wherever they like with impunity.

Screw that. Any advert in public space that gives you no choice whether you see it or not is yours. It's yours to take, re-arrange and re-use. You can do whatever you like with it. Asking for permission is like asking to keep a rock someone just threw at your head.

You owe the companies nothing. You especially don't owe them any courtesy. They have re-arranged the world to put themselves in front of you. They never asked for your permission, don't even start asking for theirs.

Poster for Greenpeace campaign against deforestation

You can't beat the feelin'

You told that joke twice

We can't do anything to change the world until
capitalism crumbles. In the meantime we should
all go shopping to console ourselves.

This painting proved too rude for the street and every reach got cleaned off within a few days. All except one on the shutter of a shop that opens until nine o'clock every night.

The only time you see the picture is after the watershed when they close. Which the boss enforces more strictly than any TV executive.

We don't need any more heroes, we just need someone to take out the recycling

A lot of mothers will do anything for their children, except let them be themselves

Bomb Middle England
People who get up early in the morning cause
war, death and famine

Street Sculpture

If you want someone to be ignored then build a lifesize bronze statue of them and stick it in the middle of town.

It doesn't matter how great you were, it'll always take an unfunny drunk with climbing skills to make people notice you.

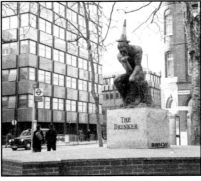

Bronze statue with bronze traffic cone

Boudicca with wheel clamp, 2005. Lasted 12 days

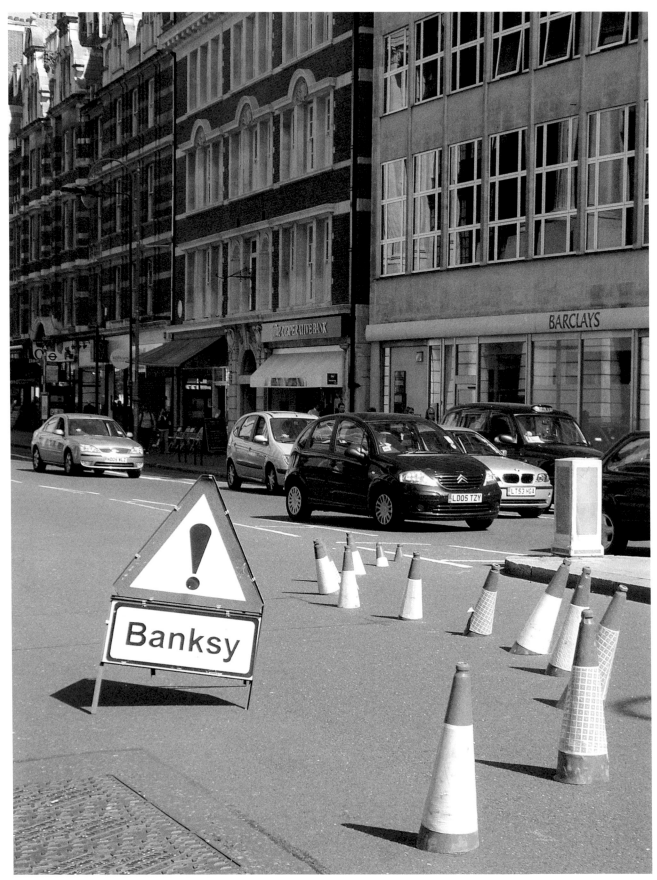

Southampton Row, London 2005. Lasted one day

Edgeware Rd, London 2005. Lasted six days

McDonalds is stealing our children.

Balloon tethered to lampost with blow-up doll,
Picadilly Circus 2004. Lasted nine hours until
she lost pressure and was hit by a bus.

After spending months thinking I was clever painting a picture of crows attacking cctv cameras I found real plastic birds in a joke shop for six pounds each.

'I heard they was put there by the police so you look up and a computer can scan your face' a stallholder on Portobello market told me when I was taking photographs.

Shoreditch High Street, lasted 4 weeks. Portobello Road, 6 weeks. Tottenham Court Road, 2 weeks

Bathing lake, Hyde Park, London 2005. Lasted 3½ weeks

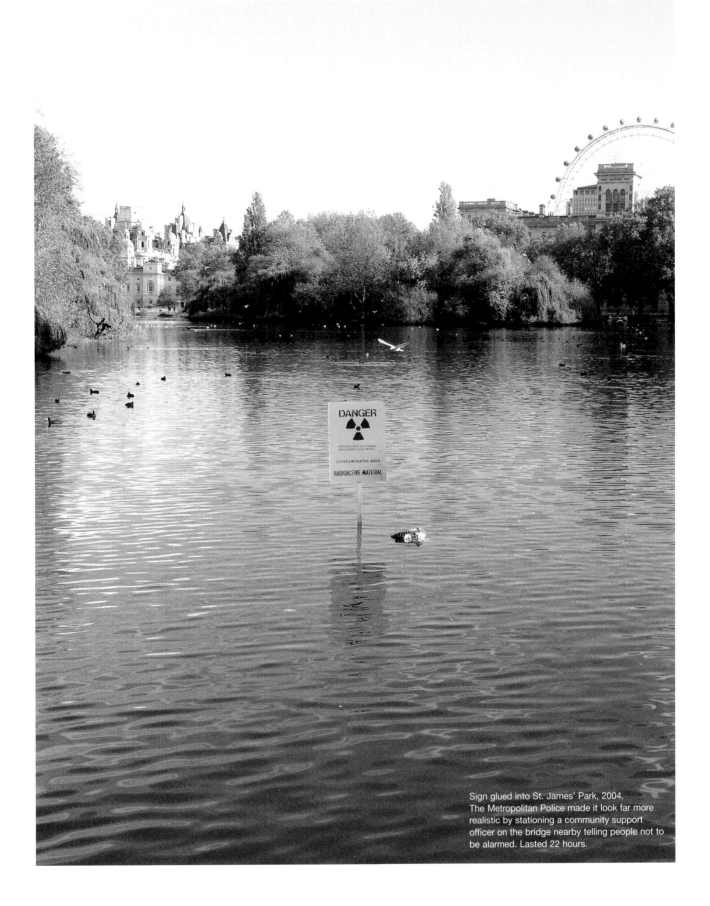

Sign glued into St. James' Park, 2004.
The Metropolitan Police made it look far more
realistic by stationing a community support
officer on the bridge nearby telling people not to
be alarmed. Lasted 22 hours.

Glastonbury Festival, 2005

Victoria Park, London 2005. Lasted 3 months

AUTHORISED GRAFFITI AREA

BY ORDER NATIONAL HIGHWAYS AGENCY
APPLIES TO STICKERED SURFACE ONLY
EU DIRECTIVE 016/BNK/5Y

YOU DONT HAVE TO BE AN ILLEGAL IMMIGRANT TO WORK HERE – BUT IT HELPS

PUT A MENU THROUGH THIS LETTERBOX AND I WILL NEVER EAT YOUR FOOD AGAIN

GUARDED 24 HOURS

By a drowsy fat bloke reading pornography

SLOW CHILDREN

Don't believe the type

WAR

Stop the War Coalition
NOT IN MY NAME

DON'T
ATTACK IRAQ

WRONG WAR

...topwar.org.uk

War Coalition
DON'T
ATTACK
IRAQ

People in glass houses shouldn't throw stones
And people in glass cities shouldn't fire missiles

Anti-war demonstration, London 2003

Modified billboard, Los Angeles 2002

Fire extinguisher with pink paint. Southbank, London 2004

Manifesto

Extract from the diary of Lieutenant Colonel Mervin Willett Gonin DSO who was amongst the first British soldiers to arrive at the Nazi death camp Bergen-Belsen. It was liberated in April 1945 close to the end of the second World War.

I can give no adequate discription of the Horror Camp in which my men and myself were to spend the next month of our lives. It was just a barren wilderness, as bare as a chicken run. Corpses lay everywhere, some in huge piles, sometimes they lay singly or in pairs where they had fallen.

It took a little time to get used to seeing men women and childen collapse as you walked by them and to restrain oneself from going to their assistance. One had to get used early to the idea that the individual just did not count. One knew that five hundred a day were dying and that five hundred a day were going on dying for weeks before anything we could do would have the slightest effect. It was, however, not easy to watch a child choking to death from diptheria when you knew a tracheotomy and nursing would save it, one saw women drowning in their own vomit because they were too weak to turn over, and men eating worms as they clutched a half loaf of bread purely because they had had to eat worms to live and now could scarcely tell the difference.

Piles of corpses, naked and obscene, with a woman too weak to stand proping herself against them as she cooked the food we had given her over an open fire; men and women crouching down just anywhere in the open relieving themselves of the dysentary which was scouring their bowels, a woman standing stark naked washing herself with some issue soap in water from a tank in which the remains of a child floated.

It was shortly after the British Red Cross arrived, though it may have no connection, that a very large quantity of lipstick arrived. This was not at all what we men wanted, we were screaming for hundreds and thousands of other things and I don't know who asked for lipstick. I wish so much that I could discover who did it, it was the action of genious, sheer unadulterated brilliance. I believe nothing did more for those internees than the lipstick. Women lay in bed with no sheets and no nightie but with scarlet red lips, you saw them wandering about with nothing but a blanket over their shoulders, but with scarlet red lips. I saw a woman dead on the post mortem table and clutched in her hand was a piece of lipstick. At last someone had done something to make them individuals again, they were someone, no longer merely the number tatooed on the arm. At last they could take an interest in their appearance. That lipstick started to give them back their humanity.

Source: Imperial War museum

Advice on making stencils

- Mindless vandalism can take a bit of thought.

- Nothing in the world is more common than unsuccessful people with talent, leave the house before you find something worth staying in for.

- Think from outside the box, collapse the box and take a fucking sharp knife to it.

- A regular 400ml can of paint will give you up to 50 A4 sized stencils. This means you can become incredibly famous/unpopular in a small town virtually overnight for approximately ten pounds.

- Try to avoid painting in places where they still point at aeroplanes.

- Spray the paint sparingly onto the stencil from a distance of 8 inches.

- When explaining yourself to the Police its worth being as reasonable as possible. Graffiti writers are not real villains. I'm always reminded of this by real villains who consider the idea of breaking in someplace, not stealing anything and then leaving behind a painting of your name in four foot high letters the most retarded thing they ever heard of.

- Be aware that going on a major mission totally drunk out of your head will result in some truly spectacular artwork and at least one night in the cells.

- The easiest way to become invisible is to wear a day-glo vest and carry a tiny transistor radio playing Heart FM very loudly. If questioned about the legitimacy of your painting simply complain about the hourly rate.

- Crime against property is not real crime. People look at an oil painting and admire the use of brushstrokes to convey meaning. People look at a graffiti painting and admire the use of a drainpipe to gain access.

- The time of getting fame for your name on its own is over. Artwork that is only about wanting to be famous will never make you famous. Fame is a by-product of doing something else. You don't go to a restaurant and order a meal because you want to have a shit.

Additional words and inspiration by
Simon Munnery, Dirty Mark, Mike Tyler,
BC Princess, Crap Hound, Brian Haw,
Tom Wolfe and D.

Additional photography by Steve Lazarides,
James Pfaff, Andy Phipps, Maya Hyuk, Aiko
and Tristan Manco.

Technical support by Eine, Farmer, Luke,
Tinks, Faile, Kev, Paul Insect, Wissam,
Jonesy and Brooksy.

Layout by Jez Tucker.

www.banksy.co.uk

Dedicated to the memory of Casual T

People either love me or they hate me, or they don't really care